Love Omnia Munda Mundis
Ginet Sosemito

Si Vales Valeo
If you are well, I am well

Love Omnia Munda Mundis

Ginet Sosemito

Copyright © 2011 Ginet Sosemito

This book and parts thereof may not be reproduced in any form or by any means, mechanical or electronic, including photocopying, recording, or by any information storage and retrieval system, without previous permission in writing from the publishers.

ISBN 978 90 820451 0 9

Registered ISBN in the Kingdom of the Netherlands.

Copy deposited with the Royal Library of the Netherlands, The Hague, Archive of Dutch Cultural Heritage

Published by Ginet Sosemito

First Edition 2013

Si Vales Valeo

Thunderstorm

Breath

The Senses

Dream

The Present

The Stars

Love

Time

Vitality

The Moment

Wonder

The Ring

Take a Note

Success

Why

One

The Smile

The Mystery

The Cheek

Feel

Love

Friendship

Exhilarate

The Perfection Point

The Chain

The Ring

Destiny

Movement & Mobility

To dwell within the heart of the world

Is much like observing a thunderstorm

One of bewildered measures

Taking you by the hand

Through time and travel

Where seas know not

Of woes,

The Seafarer captured

Or perhaps it is those ashore capturing others

Attempting to replace that Life

which is supposed to be their own

Who is the capturer and who is the captive

And who has given one ruling over the other

The Seas prefer to be their own

What is it that you feel when you breathe

What is it that you observe when you breathe,

Of your breath alone.

Tell me, is it real

Is it touchable

Is it the essence of your soul

To know is to dream

To dream is to know

How you feel

What you want

From life,

In retrospective.

For an artist

There is a social surrounding,

A being and state of mind from where you create.

A now.

From self -awareness -

Being influenced,

By the present and presence,

Of social and political impact,

Leaving an emotional response.

Stars, Jupiter and Mars

When one truly embraces oneself,

Love,

And see the beauty of self

To love your inner being,

To be

To make a change,

A change in the world

To be

In coexistence with what is,

What,

Is a given,

As life and wonders of the world surround us,

Stars- Jupiter and Mars.

Gold

Time translated into gold

Each minute is a bar of gold

Value with whom you share

Identify the receiver

as one who values the bar of gold

Your time,

Time,

Is a given

Time is Gold.

Our identity is our own,

Not to be identified with others,

Circumstances or people.

It is yours only,

You have the copyright to self.

When we see and fully embrace it as our own,

We keep our energy to our own,

Being,

There where it belongs,

There where it will give you energy,

Yourself

Strength and vitality

That which you need to carry on,

Remember you are the one that has to carry yourself,

In full vibrant energy of self.

Moments should be valued

Opposed to counting the minutes

Or months

Years even

When you might see a loved one again

Or realise the dreams you so aspire

In transition to the next,

That which is next,

That which has your name on it.

In Life, Life itself

Now that I have freed myself from you

I wonder if I may be yours.

Symbolism

In heart

In mind

Of true love

Of self

Is without measure

And to be found

In that,

Which encompasses you.

The ring of existence.

In the essence of being we know,

We know how and when to seek in self,

For answers,

Answers to the now unknown.

What are we capable of

What is it that we seek -

What we seek,

Is the turning point of not feeling the need to seek,

Rather to find the courage to belong to self,

To be our own,

To be who we are, to be in existence.

In the essence of self we are all pure.

Purity comes from self,

Take a note of the pure things of life

Of self, take a note, take notice, of self

For you are worthy and beyond that,

which was for a long time not seen

Your inner self.

Poverty in perception by others which is not yours

will lead to self discovery when you make way,

Discovery will reveal your path.

It takes courage to want to discover,

To truly dive within your own soul

While riding the bus

Or tending to life

Discover the thoughts that are not there.

Once landed in the nowhere of thoughts

There you will find the key

To the secret to self,

You yourself hold the secret

To your own being

Your soul.

To Success.

Why, is a question too many times asked.

Feel the need to be,

You,

You

Me

Therefore lies,

Within

Soul

Love

Love for self

I love you

Why is it that in thought and mind we are one

Existence

To lead to self,

Smile

A smile will fill your moment

Your cup of laughter

Your Sense of laughter when you smile

It will brighten your day

And the one after.

Joy

To be in mere existence

Mere existence

Is

To be.

A Soul's sole purpose is love.

Love and be loved.

Be loved and Love.

I lie in your arms and breathe.

Is it possible to feel love coming forth from an encounter

With the one

For the love itself being a separate entity entirely,

That love

The existence of knowing,

I call it love,

A knowing of strength, Empowerment

That exalts,

Evolves,

from knowing the other,

From knowing his being,

His existence,

His presence without distance so near.

And yet, Oceans away.

Inside my soul,

My soul responds and inhibitions disappear if there were any.

If I were to think my thoughts through

wouldn't I get buried under the weight

I dared to and captured my self, my being and my soul

And it was a Cool Breeze which struck my Cheek

Like Fall

Or a Lake waiting to be rippled by exactly those thoughts

And a Breeze was created

The one who Brushed my Cheek

Think, breathe & be Love,

Don't judge, just breathe,

Be & Love.

Synergy with self is truly a wonderful thing

It means contentment, not moderately,

But rather in a universal sense of being,

Feeling complete bliss with self,

Enjoying the surrounding,

The people - the energy,

Not demanding or expecting,

Just to be free to give and receive

For in freedom of being lies the reward itself.

In the dignity of our heart,

Our soul, mind

Lies the shape of Peace and sensibility

to acknowledge ones own unique being,

And the essence of Dignity and Grace.

Find food for your inner self - pure food of love

for your inner self,

Be foremost your own supplier.

Friendship is found in the smile from soul to soul.

Success lies in the connection with people,

In the connection itself,

In the connection itself lies a freedom to respond from self,

Creating inner awareness to freedom of and in growth socially,

Professionally in business and that which we do best,

Friendships,

And response to Self.

To bask in ones own existence is a skill.

Limitations are contributed to upbringing,

And a past environment which was not mine.

A woman her focus point of perfection

is to find a man his focus point of perfection.

Liberty

By breaking the chain of that which we,

When finding purity of self,

Will know of

How to break free of,

We are able to liberate ourselves.

Seek purity always

In self & life, feel the air around you

And touch the magic,

Of life & self, see your gift, embrace it and live it.

Love itself is touchable, in the fragrance of life.

Not the object of which you focus on when referring to love,

For your loved one is not an object

Of which love can be demanded

Or expected, or claimed.

Only in freedom love abides,

Freedom in the sense of a realm, a realm which can be

Discovered when breathing and finding silence.

The silent chambers of you.

In my solitude I find the silence of my existence.

There where my soul abides

There where my soul lies unified

With the universe in silence, while the dynamics

of my life come pulsating through my own existence.

To respond from soul

For there is where the union lies

In truly getting involved.

To dare to stand up in that freedom of our soul

Where compassion lies and unconditional love.

Not expecting but simplifying.

To entwine in bone structure,

Is it a formation of that which we feel

Or the unseen, rather a sense

Of belonging to know, where one should be

The formation in every sense

Is not to grasp, rather merge into the idea

As you are the part, that holds destiny of self.

Inflictions of the heart, Inflictions of the soul

In upbringing, are captivated in captivity

Free the soul

Free to step into the soul

There where the heart is

Claim your own Heart for it is Yours

Not the up-bringer

To release the depth of heart and soul of negligence

claimed in non-activities by others

And make way

For the soul

In all its purity

Destined to be whole.

How is it possible that he can,

Take me to this place

Within my soul

The place in my soul where I dare touch

And set foot in the gentle side

Of self, of me

There evolves a sound, what a wondrous effect

And joy of promise it holds.

I discovered that spirituality is three dimensional.

You can be meditating and be connected to the Universe

While continuing that which you must do

And needs to be done to pick up the pace,

To reality and mortality

Which encompasses riches of self,

In movement and inner creation

Which lies inside you and is yours.

Your own true wealth, yourself,

the next level

Of coexistence

Daily life and the Universe,

They are one

We give and take the time,

To observe and comprehend

This given

You will feel it, complete bliss

Joy within

It takes silence and true meditation

To reach your inner self

Don't get distracted, rather coincide with life,

To find true fulfilment one must seek the balance

Of spirituality and the unification of self in life.

Synergy with self is of uttermost importance

To adjust in the rebirth of self

To take full control of your life, yours, you.

Love Omnia Munda Mundis

Ginet Sosemito

Ginet Sosemito studied the Arts and started her own business in Europe after studies in the United States of America.
The cultures of Europe and the Americas formed the inspiration to a vision of Life, Earth and the People in Life and Love where often people are found to think love is about owning one another with much ado about nothing daily activities rather than reaching within ones own Soul where creativity and a bliss of Self is to be found. The substance of mankind's essence on this Planet in order to see not only its own orbital matter, is Love.

www.ingramcontent.com/pod-product-compliance
Lightning Source LLC
Chambersburg PA
CBHW071752090426
42738CB00011B/2665